Sea Lions

written and photographed by Frank Staub

Lerner Publications Company • Minneapolis, Minnesota

For Doctor Vaughan, Doctor Oplinger, and the Muhlenberg College Biology Department

The author wishes to acknowledge Miami Seaquarium, Oregon Coast Aquarium, Friends of the Sea Lion Marine Mammal Center, and Steve Aitchison. Special thanks to Dr. Sarah Mesnick and Dr. Carolyn Heath for helping with the research and checking the manuscript for accuracy.

Additional photographs are reproduced with the permission of: © Frank S. Balthis, pp. 17, 43; © Friends of the Sea Lion Marine Mammal Center, p. 42.

Thanks to our series consultant, Sharyn Fenwick, elementary science/math specialist. Mrs. Fenwick was the winner of the National Science Teachers Association 1991 Distinguished Teaching Award. She also was the recipient of the Presidential Award for Excellence in Math and Science Teaching, representing the state of Minnesota at the elementary level in 1992.

Early Bird Nature Books were conceptualized by Ruth Berman and designed by Steve Foley. Series editor is Joelle Riley.

Lerner Publications Company
A Division of Lerner Publishing Group
241 First Avenue North
Minneapolis, MN 55401 U.S.A.

Website address: www.lernerbooks.com

Library of Congress Cataloging-in-Publication Data

Staub, Frank J.
   Sea lions / written and photographed by Frank Staub.
     p.   cm. — (Early bird nature books)
   Summary: Describes the physical characteristics, behavior, and habitat of the California sea lion.
   ISBN 0–8225–3018–X (alk. paper)
   1. Sea lions—Juvenile literature. [1. Sea lions.] I. Title.
II. Series.
QL737.P63S725 2000
599.79'75—dc21   99-20189

Manufactured in the United States of America
1 2 3 4 5 6 – JR – 05 04 03 02 01 00

Contents

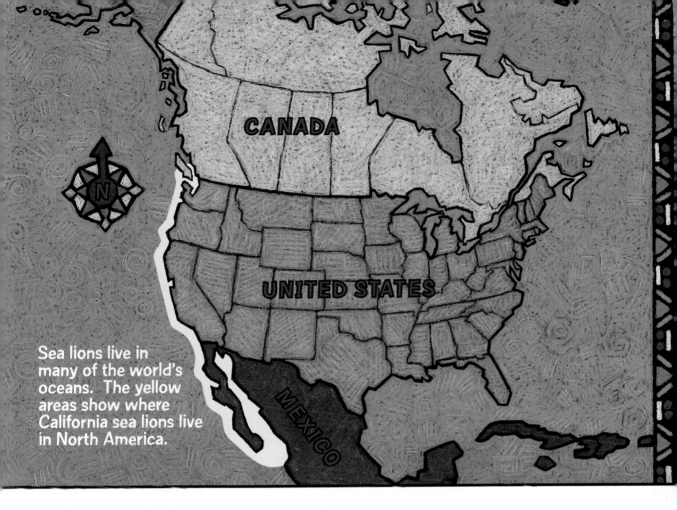

Sea lions live in many of the world's oceans. The yellow areas show where California sea lions live in North America.

CANADA

UNITED STATES

MEXICO

Be a Word Detective

Can you find these words as you read about the sea lion's life? Be a detective and try to figure out what they mean. You can turn to the glossary on page 46 for help.

blubber	nurses	rookery
colony	pinnipeds	streamlined
hauling out	predators	territory
mammals	prey	

This California sea lion is doing tricks at an aquarium. Where do most sea lions live?

On Land and at Sea

Sea lions look a lot like seals. Some sea lions live in zoos and aquariums. But most sea lions are wild animals. They live in the ocean and along its shores.

Most California sea lions live in North America, along the shore of the Pacific Ocean.

Sea lions are in a group of animals called pinnipeds (PIH-nuh-pehdz). There are three families of pinnipeds. Sea lions are in the eared seal family. The other two families of pinnipeds are earless seals and walruses. Eared seals have pointed ears. Earless seals and walruses have ears too. But their ears are just holes on the sides of their head.

The walrus is the only pinniped with tusks. But all pinnipeds have whiskers.

Harbor seals are earless seals. Their flippers are all about the same size.

Pinnipeds don't have arms or legs. Instead, they have four flippers. Eared seals and walruses have two long front flippers. They have two shorter back flippers. All four of an earless seal's flippers are about the same size.

California sea lions have three nails on each of their back flippers. The scientific name of the California sea lion is Zalophus californianus.

Pinnipeds use their flippers to move around on land. Eared seals and walruses can walk. Their front flippers hold them up. And they can turn their back flippers forward. They walk

When California sea lions walk, they swing their heads from side to side. On land, a sea lion can move as fast as a person.

on all four flippers. Earless seals' front flippers do not hold them up. And they can't turn their back flippers forward. So earless seals can't walk. They just scoot along on their bellies.

*There are five different kinds of sea lions. California sea lions
can be up to 8 feet long and weigh up to 800 pounds.*

Pinnipeds also use their flippers to swim.
Eared seals pull themselves through the water
with their front flippers. They use their head

and neck to steer. Earless seals and walruses swim differently from eared seals. They use their front flippers for steering. Their back flippers push them through the water.

California sea lions use their strong front flippers to pull themselves through the water.

Chapter 2

This California sea lion's nostrils are open. Sea lions close their nostrils when they go underwater. Can sea lions breathe underwater?

Like Underwater Bullets

California sea lions swim a lot. But they can't breathe underwater. Sea lions must swim to the water's surface to breathe air. That's because sea lions are mammals. Mammals are animals who breathe air, have hair, and drink their mother's milk.

Sea lions stay in the water for hours at a time. Ocean water can be cold. A sea lion's hair and blubber keep it warm. Blubber is a thick layer of fat just under a sea lion's skin. Blubber wraps around a sea lion like a coat. And the sea lion's hair keeps cold water off its skin.

This California sea lion is holding its flippers together. This is called a jug handle because the flippers look like the handle of a jug.

A sea lion's body is streamlined. A streamlined body is smooth and rounded. It moves easily through water. A sea lion's streamlined body helps it to swim fast. Sea lions can shoot through the water like bullets.

California sea lions usually swim about 15 miles per hour. But they can swim as fast as 25 miles per hour.

These California sea lions are chasing fish. Sea lions use their sharp teeth to bite into their prey.

Sea lions must swim to find food. They are predators. Predators are animals who hunt and eat other animals. The animals that a predator hunts are called its prey. A sea lion's prey is usually fish or squid.

After swimming and hunting, sea lions rest. Groups of sea lions float together on the water's surface. From far away, resting sea lions look like a raft made of logs.

These California sea lions look like a floating raft. Inset: Sea lions often hold up their flippers while they float.

Chapter 3

This California sea lion is about to leave the water. What is it called when a sea lion pulls itself onto the land?

Resting on Land

California sea lions often leave the water. They pull themselves onto the land with their flippers. This is called hauling out. Most sea lions haul out on islands. Some haul out on big rocks that stick out of the water.

Some of the California sea lions in this colony just hauled out. Their wet hair looks dark and shiny.

While sea lions are on land, they live in a group. This group is called a colony. Male and female sea lions usually stay away from each other. So colonies often have places for only males or only females.

Sea lions sleep on land. It is warmer on land than in the water. Sometimes a sea lion gets too warm on land. Then it needs to cool off. A sea lion cools off by lifting its head or a flipper up in the air. The fresh air cools the sea lion. But if the sea lion is still too hot, it goes into the water.

California sea lions sleep most of the time they are on land.

Sea lions usually rest near each other on land. They often lie pressed together. So sometimes a sea lion feels crowded. Then it argues with its neighbors. It argues to tell other sea lions that it needs more space.

When California sea lions sleep, they often lie on or next to other sea lions.

These California sea lions are arguing. Sea lions bark to talk to each other.

When a sea lion argues, it opens its mouth wide. It shakes its head and barks loudly. Sea lion arguments last for only a few seconds. But they happen many times each day. So sea lion colonies are noisy places.

Chapter 4

Male California sea lions have a large bump on their foreheads. This bump is called a crest. Where do males live in late spring?

Bull Fights

Adult male sea lions are called bulls. In late spring, most California sea lion bulls go to the part of the colony where females live. The bulls set up territories. A territory is an area that an animal keeps for itself. Some bulls have territories on rocks in the water. But most bulls have territories on beaches.

Bulls fight other bulls to set up territories. The bulls push with their chests and bite one another. A bull's hair and blubber help to protect it from being badly bitten. A fight ends when one bull gives up and leaves.

Not all bulls have territories. But all bulls fight.

Bulls only fight other bulls. They fight any bull who tries to take over their territory. Females can go in and out of a bull's territory. But other bulls have to stay out.

Many females are in this California sea lion bull's territory. A bull's territory is usually about the size of a school bus.

When the pup is less than one week old, its mother leaves. She goes to the ocean to hunt. She may be gone for days. When she comes back, she barks for her pup. Sometimes more than one pup comes to her. But she knows her own pup by its smell and its voice.

A newborn California sea lion pup is up to 3 feet long and weighs up to 35 pounds.

Territories usually include both land and water. These bulls are fighting over a territory.

A bull stays in his territory day and night. The bull doesn't eat while he guards his territory. After a few weeks he is very hungry. Then he leaves to hunt in the ocean. While he is gone, another bull takes his territory. When the bull returns to shore, he must fight if he wants a new territory.

These California sea lion females and babies are resting near the water. What is the name of the area where babies are born?

Raising Pups

Adult female sea lions are called cows. California sea lion cows have babies in late spring and early summer. Babies are born in an area called a rookery. Most rookeries are on small islands.

A cow has one baby at a time. The baby sea lion is called a pup. The pup can walk soon after it is born. During its first days of life, the pup stays with its mother and nurses often. Nursing is drinking mother's milk.

This newborn California sea lion pup is nursing. Sea lions' milk has twice as much fat as ice cream.

A cow barks to call her pup. A pup learns its mother's voice soon after birth.

The pup nurses when its mother returns. It nurses as much as it can, because after a few days its mother will go hunting again.

Most California sea lion pups grow up in the same rookery where their mothers grew up.

While the mother is away, her pup sleeps a lot. It also plays with other pups whose mothers are gone. The pups wrestle, chase, and bite each other. Sometimes pups seem to argue just like adults.

When pups play, they seem to argue like adults.

The newborn pup cannot swim. It splashes in pools of water along the beach. It watches other sea lions swimming. When it is about two weeks old, the pup tries to swim.

This California sea lion pup is learning to swim by watching its mother.

Territories usually include both land and water.
These bulls are fighting over a territory.

A bull stays in his territory day and night.
The bull doesn't eat while he guards his
territory. After a few weeks he is very hungry.
Then he leaves to hunt in the ocean. While he
is gone, another bull takes his territory. When
the bull returns to shore, he must fight if he
wants a new territory.

These California sea lion females and babies are resting near the water. What is the name of the area where babies are born?

Raising Pups

Adult female sea lions are called cows. California sea lion cows have babies in late spring and early summer. Babies are born in an area called a rookery. Most rookeries are on small islands.

A cow has one baby at a time. The baby sea lion is called a pup. The pup can walk soon after it is born. During its first days of life, the pup stays with its mother and nurses often. Nursing is drinking mother's milk.

This newborn California sea lion pup is nursing. Sea lions' milk has twice as much fat as ice cream.

When the pup is less than one week old, its mother leaves. She goes to the ocean to hunt. She may be gone for days. When she comes back, she barks for her pup. Sometimes more than one pup comes to her. But she knows her own pup by its smell and its voice.

A newborn California sea lion pup is up to 3 feet long and weighs up to 35 pounds.

A cow barks to call her pup. A pup learns its mother's voice soon after birth.

The pup nurses when its mother returns. It nurses as much as it can, because after a few days its mother will go hunting again.

Most California sea lion pups grow up in the same rookery where their mothers grew up.

While the mother is away, her pup sleeps a lot. It also plays with other pups whose mothers are gone. The pups wrestle, chase, and bite each other. Sometimes pups seem to argue just like adults.

When pups play, they seem to argue like adults.

The newborn pup cannot swim. It splashes in pools of water along the beach. It watches other sea lions swimming. When it is about two weeks old, the pup tries to swim.

This California sea lion pup is learning to swim by watching its mother.

When pups are learning to swim, they spend a lot of time playing in shallow water.

When the pup is about six weeks old, it can swim well. But it can't stay in the water long. Its blubber is too thin to keep it warm.

As the pup grows, its blubber becomes thicker. Thick blubber keeps the pup warm. So the pup can spend more time in the water.

As California sea lion pups grow, they spend more and more time in the water and underwater.

When the pup is four months old, it can swim as well as its mother. It can stay underwater for five minutes or longer.

The pup spends less and less time with its mother. It spends more time exploring the rookery. When the pup is six months old, it can catch its own food. But usually it nurses too. When the pup is about one year old, it leaves its mother and lives on its own.

Most California sea lion pups stay with their mother until they are about one year old.

Chapter 6

These California sea lion bulls are going into the ocean. Do sea lions have enemies that live in the ocean?

Dangers to Sea Lions

California sea lions are not hunted by land animals. But they do have enemies in the water. Sharks and killer whales hunt swimming sea lions.

When a shark attacks, it usually bites just once. It does not hold onto the sea lion. The shark waits for the sea lion to bleed to death. If the bite isn't deep, the sea lion may be able to swim away. But sharks often kill old, young, or sick sea lions. These sea lions are too weak to get away.

This bull was probably bitten by a shark.

This California sea lion pup was playing with a fishing net. The net became stuck around the pup's neck.

People sometimes hurt sea lions too. Some of the chemicals (KEH-mih-kuhlz) people use on land go into the ocean. Chemicals in the water can make sea lions sick.

Many people use nets to catch fish. Young sea lions often play with the fishing nets. Sometimes part of a fishing net gets stuck around a young sea lion's neck. As the sea lion grows, the net becomes tighter. The net may tear off. Or the sea lion may be able to rub it off against a rock. But if the net stays on, it begins to cut into the sea lion's skin.

Some people put noisemakers on their fishing nets. The noisemakers make noises that scare sea lions. So sea lions don't play with nets that have noisemakers.

Sometimes fishing nets tear off of a sea lion's neck. The net tore off of this California sea lion cow's neck, but the wound has not healed yet.

Other people take sick and injured sea lions to sea lion hospitals. People at the hospitals feed the sea lions. They cut fishing nets from the sea lions' bodies. They give medicine to sick sea lions. The sea lions are cared for until they are healthy. Then people return the sea lions to the ocean.

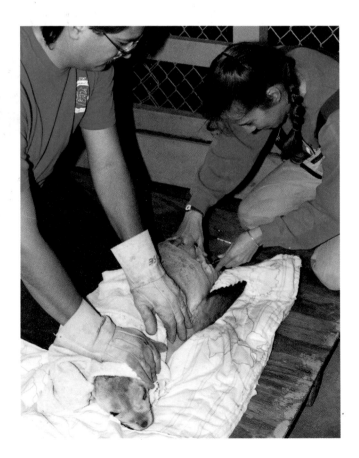

These people are giving medicine to a sick sea lion. When the sea lion is healthy, it will be returned to the ocean.

People have made laws to protect sea lions. The sign in this picture reminds people to obey the laws.

There are many healthy California sea lions. Some people work to protect them. When you grow up, maybe you will help to protect sea lions too.

On Sharing a Book

As you know, adults greatly influence a child's attitude toward reading. When a child sees you read, or when you share a book with a child, you're sending a message that reading is important. Show the child that reading a book together is important to you. Find a comfortable, quiet place. Turn off the television and limit other distractions, such as telephone calls.

Be prepared to start slowly. Take turns reading parts of this book. Stop and talk about what you're reading. Talk about the photographs. You may find that much of the shared time is spent discussing just a few pages. This discussion time is valuable for both of you, so don't move through the book too quickly. If the child begins to lose interest, stop reading. Continue sharing the book at another time. When you do pick up the book again, be sure to revisit the parts you have already read. Most importantly, enjoy the book!

Be a Vocabulary Detective

You will find a word list on page 5. Words selected for this list are important to the understanding of the topic of this book. Encourage the child to be a word detective and search for the words as you read the book together. Talk about what the words mean and how they are used in the sentence. Do any of these words have more than one meaning? You will find these words defined in a glossary on page 46.

What about Questions?

Use questions to make sure the child understands the information in this book. Here are some suggestions:

> What did this paragraph tell us? What does this picture show? What do you think we'll learn about next? What does a sea lion look like? Where do sea lions live? Where do sea lions catch their food? How do sea lions stay warm? How do they stay cool? How do sea lions talk? How long does a baby sea lion stay with its mother? What dangers do sea lions face? How are sea lions like people? How are they different? What do you think it's like to be a sea lion? What is your favorite part of the book? Why?

If the child has questions, don't hesitate to respond with questions of your own such as: What do *you* think? Why? What is it that you don't know? If the child can't remember certain facts, turn to the index.

44

Introducing the Index

The index is an important learning tool. It helps readers get information quickly without searching throughout the whole book. Turn to the index on page 47. Choose an entry, such as *flippers,* and ask the child to use the index to find out how a sea lion uses its flippers. Repeat this exercise with as many entries as you like. Ask the child to point out the differences between an index and a glossary. (The index helps readers find information quickly, while the glossary tells readers what words mean.)

All the World in Metric!

Although our monetary system is in metric units (based on multiples of 10), the United States is one of the few countries in the world that does not use the metric system of measurement. Here are some conversion activities you and the child can do using a calculator:

WHEN YOU KNOW:	MULTIPLY BY:	TO FIND:
miles	1.609	kilometers
feet	0.3048	meters
inches	2.54	centimeters
gallons	3.787	liters
tons	0.907	metric tons
pounds	0.454	kilograms

Activities

Look at the picture of the sea lion's ear on page 30. Touch your ears. How are your ears like sea lion ears? How are they different? Look at the picture of a sea lion's front flipper on page 10. Then look at your own hand and arm. How are your hand and arm like the flipper? How are they different?

Think about what sea lions need to be healthy. Make up a story about the daily life of sea lions. Be sure to include information from this book. Draw or paint pictures to illustrate your story.

Walk like a sea lion. Next, crawl on your belly like a seal. Which way is easier? Which way do you move faster? Have a friend crawl like a seal while you walk like a sea lion. Race and see who wins.

Glossary

blubber—the thick layer of fat just under a sea lion's skin

colony—a group of sea lions who live together on land

hauling out—a sea lion pulling its body onto land

mammals—animals who breathe air, have hair, and drink their mother's milk

nurses—drinks mother's milk

pinnipeds—ocean animals that have four flippers

predators—animals that hunt and eat other animals

prey—animals that a predator hunts and eats

rookery—area where baby sea lions are born and raised

streamlined—smooth and rounded. A streamlined body moves through water easily.

territory—area that an animal keeps for itself

Index

Pages listed in **bold** type refer to photographs.

The Early Bird Nature Books Series